Mastering SAP Master Data Governance (MDG): A Guide to Data Management and Governance

Table of Contents:

Chapter 1: Introduction to SAP Master Data Governance

Chapter 2: Setting up SAP Master Data Governance

Chapter 3: Master Data Governance Processes

Chapter 4: Data Modeling and Consolidation

Chapter 5: Business Rules and Validations

Chapter 6: User Interfaces and Data Governance Framework

Chapter 7: Data Quality Management

Chapter 8: Integration and Extensibility

Chapter 9: Master Data Consolidation and Harmonization

Chapter 10: Data Migration Strategies

Chapter 11: Data Maintenance and Ongoing Data Governance

Chapter 12: Data Migration Strategies

Chapter 13: Reporting and Analytics

Chapter 14: Integration with Other Systems

Chapter 1: Introduction to SAP Master Data Governance

Welcome to Chapter 1 of "Mastering SAP Master Data Governance (MDG): A Comprehensive Guide to Data Management and Governance." In this chapter, we will provide you with an introduction to SAP Master Data Governance and its significance in the world of data management. Let's get started!

Section 1.1: Understanding the Importance of Master Data Governance

Master data is the critical business information that describes various entities such as customers, suppliers, products, and employees. Managing this master data efficiently and ensuring its quality is crucial for organizations to make informed business decisions, improve operational efficiency, and maintain regulatory compliance.

Master Data Governance (MDG) is a comprehensive solution provided by SAP that enables organizations to establish a centralized and standardized framework for managing their master data. SAP MDG helps in creating, maintaining, and distributing consistent and reliable master data across the enterprise landscape.

Section 1.2: Overview of SAP Master Data Governance (MDG)

SAP MDG offers a wide range of features and functionalities to support end-to-end master data management processes. Here are some key aspects of SAP MDG:

Centralized Data Governance: SAP MDG provides a single point of control for managing master data, ensuring data consistency and integrity across systems.

Data Quality Management: The solution offers robust data quality capabilities, allowing organizations to define and enforce data quality rules, perform data cleansing, and monitor data quality metrics.

Workflow and Approval Processes: SAP MDG supports flexible workflow and approval processes, ensuring proper governance and authorization for master data changes.

Data Consolidation and Harmonization: With SAP MDG, you can consolidate and harmonize master data from various systems, eliminating duplicates and standardizing data formats.

Integration with SAP and Non-SAP Systems: SAP MDG seamlessly integrates with other SAP solutions like SAP ERP, CRM, and non-SAP systems, enabling data synchronization and collaboration.

Section 1.3: Key Benefits and Use Cases of SAP MDG

SAP MDG offers several benefits to organizations seeking effective master data management. Some of the key advantages include:

Data Consistency: SAP MDG ensures consistent and accurate master data across the organization, reducing data inconsistencies and errors.

Increased Efficiency: By automating master data processes and workflows, SAP MDG streamlines data management tasks, reducing manual effort and improving operational efficiency.

Regulatory Compliance: SAP MDG helps organizations adhere to regulatory requirements by maintaining accurate and auditable master data records.

Improved Decision-Making: With reliable and up-to-date master data, organizations can make informed business decisions based on accurate information.

Enhanced Customer Experience: SAP MDG enables organizations to provide a unified and consistent customer experience by ensuring accurate and consistent customer data across systems.

Section 1.4: Exploring the Architecture and Components of SAP MDG

SAP MDG comprises various components that work together to provide a comprehensive master data governance solution. The key components include:

Data Model: The data model defines the structure of master data entities and their attributes. It allows organizations to customize and extend the standard data model to meet their specific requirements.

User Interfaces: SAP MDG offers user-friendly interfaces for different user roles, such as data stewards, data administrators, and business users. These interfaces enable users to create, edit, and review master data records.

Business Rules Framework: The Business Rules Framework (BRF+) in SAP MDG allows organizations to define and implement business rules for data validation, derivation, and workflow triggering.

Workflow and Business Process Management: SAP MDG leverages the SAP Business Workflow engine for defining and executing approval workflows and business processes.

Data Replication and Synchronization: SAP MDG integrates with various SAP and non-SAP systems to ensure data consistency across the landscape. It supports mechanisms like BAPIs, IDocs, and web services for data replication.

That concludes Chapter 1: Introduction to SAP Master Data Governance. In this chapter, we provided an overview of SAP MDG, its importance, key features, benefits, and components. In the upcoming chapters, we will dive deeper into each aspect of SAP MDG to help you master the art of managing master data efficiently and effectively. Stay tuned!

Section 1.4 (Continued): Exploring the Architecture and Components of SAP MDG

SAP MDG comprises additional components that contribute to its robust architecture and functionality. Let's explore them further:

Data Quality Management: SAP MDG incorporates data quality management capabilities to ensure that master data meets defined quality standards. It enables organizations to define data quality rules, perform data cleansing, and monitor data quality metrics.

Master Data Consolidation: SAP MDG provides tools and processes for master data consolidation. It allows organizations to identify and merge duplicate or similar master data records, ensuring a single version of truth.

Governance and Stewardship: The governance and stewardship component of SAP MDG focuses on defining and enforcing data governance policies, roles, and responsibilities. It empowers data stewards to manage data quality and consistency effectively.

Integration and Extensibility: SAP MDG offers integration capabilities to connect with other systems and applications within the enterprise landscape. It supports various integration technologies, such as web services, IDocs, and APIs, to exchange data seamlessly.

Reporting and Analytics: SAP MDG provides reporting and analytics tools to monitor and evaluate master data governance processes. It offers pre-defined reports and dashboards, as well as the ability to create custom reports, enabling organizations to gain insights into data quality and governance.

Section 1.5: Conclusion

In this chapter, we provided you with an introduction to SAP Master Data Governance (MDG). We explored its significance in data management, key features and components, and the benefits it offers to organizations. SAP MDG provides a centralized and standardized approach to master data governance, ensuring data consistency, quality, and compliance across the enterprise.

In the upcoming chapters, we will delve deeper into various aspects of SAP MDG, including its configuration, data modeling, workflows, data quality management, integration, and advanced concepts. By the end of this comprehensive guide, you will have the knowledge and skills required to leverage SAP MDG effectively and master the art of managing your organization's master data.

Get ready to embark on an exciting journey of mastering SAP Master Data Governance!

Chapter 2: Setting up SAP Master Data Governance

Section 2.1: Planning and Preparation for SAP MDG Implementation

Before implementing SAP Master Data Governance (MDG), it is crucial to plan and prepare adequately. Proper planning ensures a smooth and successful implementation. In this section, we will discuss the key steps involved in planning and preparing for SAP MDG implementation.

Define Project Scope: Clearly define the scope of your SAP MDG implementation project. Identify which master data domains and processes you want to govern using SAP MDG. This step helps in determining the required resources, timelines, and deliverables.

Assemble a Project Team: Build a competent project team comprising business process experts, IT professionals, and data stewards. Assign roles and responsibilities to team members and ensure their availability throughout the project.

Assess Current State: Evaluate your existing master data management processes, systems, and data quality. Identify pain points, challenges, and opportunities for improvement. This assessment will serve as a baseline for designing the target state with SAP MDG.

Define Future State: Based on the assessment, envision the desired future state of master data management with SAP MDG. Determine the goals, objectives, and outcomes you expect to achieve. Document the business requirements and key performance indicators (KPIs) to measure success.

Infrastructure and Landscape Planning: Assess your infrastructure requirements for SAP MDG. Consider factors such as hardware, software, network, and security. Plan the system landscape architecture, including development, quality assurance, and production environments.

Data Governance Framework: Establish a data governance framework aligned with your organization's goals and objectives. Define data governance policies, roles, and responsibilities. Determine the data governance processes, workflows, and decision-making structures to be implemented.

Section 2.2: Installation and System Landscape Requirements

To install SAP Master Data Governance, you need to ensure that your system landscape meets the necessary requirements. In this section, we will cover the key aspects of system landscape requirements and the installation process.

Hardware Requirements: Review the hardware specifications recommended by SAP for the installation of SAP MDG. Consider factors such as server capacity, memory, storage, and network connectivity. Ensure that your hardware infrastructure can handle the expected workload.

Software Requirements: Determine the software components required for SAP MDG installation. This includes the operating system, database management system (DBMS), and other software dependencies. Check the compatibility matrix provided by SAP to ensure that your chosen software versions are supported.

Installation Process: Follow the installation guide provided by SAP to install SAP MDG. This involves executing installation files, configuring system parameters, and performing post-installation activities. Ensure that all prerequisites and dependencies are met before starting the installation process.

System Landscape Design: Design the system landscape for SAP MDG, considering the development, quality assurance, and production systems. Determine the transport landscape and define the system roles, such as development, consolidation, and distribution systems.

Integration Considerations: Identify the integration points between SAP MDG and other systems in your landscape. Determine the integration technologies to be used, such as web services, IDocs, or APIs. Plan the necessary configurations and mappings to enable seamless data exchange.

Section 2.3: Configuring SAP MDG: Data Modeling and Extension

Once the installation is complete, you need to configure SAP MDG according to your organization's requirements. In this section, we will focus on data modeling and extension, which involves defining the structure and attributes of master data entities in SAP MDG.

Data Model Design: Analyze your master data requirements and design the data model in SAP MDG. Identify the master data domains and entities you want to govern. Determine the attributes, relationships, and validation rules for each entity.

Entity Types and Attributes: Create entity types to represent different master data objects, such as customers, suppliers, or products. Define the attributes for each entity type, such as name, address, or contact information. Consider the data types, lengths, and value ranges for each attribute.

Relationships and Hierarchies: Define the relationships between different entities in SAP MDG. For example, a customer entity may have relationships with sales areas or contact persons. Design hierarchies, if applicable, to represent parent-child relationships between entities.

Data Validation and Derivation: Implement data validation rules to ensure data quality and consistency. Define checks, such as mandatory fields, value ranges, or pattern validations. Configure derivation rules to automatically populate certain fields based on predefined logic.

Extension Fields: SAP MDG allows you to extend the standard data model by adding custom fields. Identify the additional fields required to capture specific business data and create extension fields for the relevant entity types. Determine the data types, lengths, and validations for the extension fields.

In the next chapter, we will continue our journey by exploring the master data governance processes in SAP MDG. We will dive into the creation and maintenance of master data records, data replication, data quality management, and workflow and approval processes. Stay tuned for Chapter 3: Master Data Governance Processes.

Chapter 3: Master Data Governance Processes

Section 3.1: Creating and Maintaining Master Data Records

In this section, we will explore the processes involved in creating and maintaining master data records using SAP Master Data Governance (MDG).

Data Creation: Start by creating a new master data record in SAP MDG. Depending on the configured data model, you will be prompted to enter the required attributes and values for the selected entity type. Ensure that you provide accurate and complete information during the data creation process.

Data Maintenance: Once a master data record is created, you may need to update or modify it over time. Use the data maintenance functionality in SAP MDG to make changes to the existing records. You can edit attributes, add or remove relationships, and perform other relevant modifications as needed.

Data Validation: SAP MDG incorporates data validation mechanisms to ensure the quality and integrity of master data. During the data creation or maintenance process, the system will perform checks based on the defined validation rules. Address any validation errors or warnings and ensure that the data complies with the specified rules.

Data Approvals: In organizations with strict governance policies, data changes typically require approval from designated stakeholders or data stewards. SAP MDG supports workflow and approval processes to facilitate this. Once a master data record is created or modified, it can be sent for review and approval through predefined workflows. Ensure that the appropriate approval processes are followed and any required actions are taken.

Data Versioning: SAP MDG tracks the history of master data changes by maintaining versions of each record. This allows you to review the complete lifecycle of a record, including all modifications and approvals. Utilize the versioning functionality to access and compare previous versions of master data records, enabling better data governance and decision-making.

Section 3.2: Data Replication and Synchronization across Systems

SAP MDG enables the replication and synchronization of master data across various systems in your landscape. In this section, we will delve into the processes involved in data replication and synchronization.

Initial Data Load: When implementing SAP MDG, you will often need to perform an initial data load to populate the system with existing master data. This involves extracting data from legacy systems or other sources and transforming it into the required format for SAP MDG. Follow the defined data mapping and transformation rules to ensure accurate and complete data migration.

Data Replication: After the initial data load, ongoing data replication is necessary to keep master data consistent across systems. SAP MDG provides integration capabilities to replicate data to other SAP systems (such as SAP ERP or SAP CRM) or non-SAP systems. This can be achieved through various technologies such as BAPIs, IDocs, or web services. Configure the replication settings to determine which data should be replicated and the frequency of replication.

Data Consistency Checks: During data replication, it is crucial to perform consistency checks to ensure that the replicated data aligns with the defined data governance rules and policies. SAP MDG allows you to set up checks to validate replicated data, identifying any discrepancies or conflicts. Implement data consistency checks to maintain the integrity and accuracy of master data across systems.

Data Harmonization: In multi-system landscapes, it is common to encounter duplicate or inconsistent master data across different systems. SAP MDG offers data harmonization functionality to address this issue. By leveraging data matching and merging techniques, you can identify and merge duplicate or similar records, establishing a single version of truth for master data.

Section 3.3: Data Quality Management and Validation

Ensuring high-quality master data is a crucial aspect of effective data governance. SAP MDG provides robust data quality management and validation capabilities. Let's explore the processes involved:

Data Quality Rules: Define data quality rules in SAP MDG to enforce data quality standards. These rules can cover various aspects such as data completeness, accuracy, uniqueness, and consistency. Configure the rules based on your organization's requirements and industry best practices.

Data Cleansing: SAP MDG enables data cleansing activities to rectify data quality issues. Utilize the data cleansing functionality to identify and correct inconsistencies, errors, or redundancies in master data. This can include tasks such as address standardization, duplicate identification, or data enrichment.

Data Enrichment: SAP MDG allows you to enhance master data by enriching it with additional information. This can involve retrieving data from external sources, integrating with third-party data providers, or leveraging internal data repositories. Implement data enrichment strategies to augment the quality and completeness of master data.

Data Quality Monitoring: Continuously monitor the quality of master data using the monitoring and reporting features of SAP MDG. Generate data quality reports and metrics to assess the compliance of master data with defined quality rules. Implement proactive monitoring to identify and resolve data quality issues promptly.

Section 3.4: Workflow and Approval Processes in SAP MDG

Workflow and approval processes play a critical role in governing master data changes. SAP MDG offers robust workflow capabilities to streamline and automate these processes. Let's explore the key steps involved:

Workflow Design: Define the workflow design for master data governance processes in SAP MDG. Determine the sequence of activities, approval steps, and decision points within the workflow. Configure the workflow to align with your organization's data governance policies and approval hierarchies.

Workflow Triggers: Set up triggers to initiate the workflow for specific events or conditions. For example, a new master data record creation or a change request submission can trigger the workflow process. Define the triggering events based on your organization's requirements and data governance workflows.

Approval Steps: Configure the approval steps within the workflow to ensure proper authorization for master data changes. Define the approvers or decision-makers at each step and determine the rules for approval or rejection. The workflow should follow the defined data governance policies and procedures.

Notification and Escalation: SAP MDG allows you to send notifications to stakeholders at various stages of the workflow. Configure notifications to inform users about pending approvals, changes, or any other relevant information. Implement escalation mechanisms to handle cases where approvals are delayed or require urgent attention.

Workflow Monitoring: Monitor the progress of workflow processes using the monitoring and reporting features provided by SAP MDG. Track the status of approval requests, identify bottlenecks, and ensure timely completion of workflows. Leverage the reporting capabilities to analyze workflow performance and optimize the process if needed.

In Chapter 4, we will explore data modeling and consolidation in SAP MDG. We will discuss the configuration of entity types, relationships, and data consolidation techniques. Stay tuned for Chapter 4: Data Modeling and Consolidation.

Chapter 4: Data Modeling and Consolidation

Section 4.1: Understanding Data Models in SAP MDG

In this chapter, we will dive into data modeling and consolidation in SAP Master Data Governance (MDG). Data models form the foundation of SAP MDG and determine the structure and attributes of master data entities. Let's explore the key concepts and steps involved in data modeling.

Entity Types: Entity types represent different types of master data objects, such as customers, products, or suppliers. In SAP MDG, entity types define the structure and attributes of these objects. Identify the entity types relevant to your organization and configure them in the data model.

Attributes: Attributes define the characteristics or properties of an entity type. They capture specific information about a master data object. Determine the attributes required for each entity type, such as name, address, contact details, or classification data. Define the data types, lengths, and value ranges for each attribute.

Relationships: Relationships establish connections or associations between different master data entities. For example, a customer entity may have relationships with sales areas or contact persons. Identify the relationships relevant to your business processes and define them in the data model. Specify the cardinality, roles, and navigability of each relationship.

Data Model Extensions: SAP MDG allows you to extend the standard data model by adding custom fields or additional attributes to the entity types. Evaluate your organization's specific data requirements and determine if any custom fields need to be included. Configure the extensions to capture the additional data in the master data records.

Section 4.2: Configuring Entity Types, Attributes, and Relationships

Once you have identified the entity types, attributes, and relationships, it's time to configure them in SAP MDG. Follow these steps to set up the data model:

Entity Type Configuration: Create the entity types in SAP MDG based on your identified master data objects. Specify the attributes, relationships, and other relevant settings for each entity type. Consider the data types, lengths, and value ranges for the attributes to ensure accurate data representation.

Attribute Configuration: Define the attributes for each entity type in the data model. Determine the technical properties, such as data type, length, and domain. Configure the display properties, such as labels, descriptions, or value help options. Set up input validation rules, such as mandatory fields or value checks.

Relationship Configuration: Configure the relationships between entity types in SAP MDG. Define the relationship type, cardinality, and roles for each relationship. Specify the navigability of relationships, enabling easy navigation between connected master data records. Configure any additional properties required for relationship maintenance.

Data Model Extension: If you need to add custom fields or additional attributes to the data model, set up data model extensions. Identify the extension fields required for each entity type. Define the technical properties, such as data type, length, and domain. Configure the display properties and input validation rules for the extension fields.

Section 4.3: Data Consolidation and Harmonization Techniques

Data consolidation and harmonization are essential processes in SAP MDG to ensure consistent and reliable master data. Let's explore the key techniques involved in data consolidation:

Duplicate Detection: SAP MDG offers duplicate detection functionality to identify duplicate or similar master data records. Configure duplicate detection rules based on selected attributes and comparison criteria. Run the duplicate detection process to identify potential duplicates. Review and resolve any identified duplicates to maintain data accuracy.

Duplicate Resolution: Once duplicate records are identified, determine the resolution approach. SAP MDG provides various methods to resolve duplicates, such as merging duplicate records or selecting the most appropriate record as the survivor. Configure the duplicate resolution rules and determine the survivorship criteria. Execute the duplicate resolution process to merge or update the duplicate records.

Data Harmonization: In multi-system landscapes, data inconsistencies may exist across different systems. Data harmonization in SAP MDG aims to standardize and align master data across systems. Analyze the existing master data, identify inconsistencies or variations, and define harmonization rules. Configure the harmonization process to transform or align the data according to the defined rules.

Data Quality Checks: During data consolidation and harmonization, perform data quality checks to ensure the accuracy and completeness of master data. Define data quality rules and validations to verify the consistency and integrity of the consolidated data. Address any data quality issues identified during the checks.

In Chapter 5, we will explore business rules and validations in SAP MDG. We will discuss how to define and implement business rules, configure validations, and enforce data governance policies. Stay tuned for Chapter 5: Business Rules and Validations.

Chapter 5: Business Rules and Validations

Section 5.1: Defining and Implementing Business Rules

Business rules play a crucial role in ensuring data quality, consistency, and compliance within SAP Master Data Governance (MDG). In this chapter, we will explore the processes involved in defining and implementing business rules.

Identify Business Requirements: Start by identifying the business requirements and data governance policies that need to be enforced. Engage with stakeholders and subject matter experts to understand the specific rules and regulations that apply to your organization's master data. Document these requirements for reference during the rule definition process.

Define Rule Types: SAP MDG supports various types of business rules, such as value checks, cross-field checks, derivation rules, and workflow triggers. Determine which rule types are relevant to your business processes and data governance objectives. Each rule type serves a specific purpose and contributes to maintaining data quality and consistency.

Rule Definition: For each business rule, define the conditions, actions, and evaluation logic. Specify the attributes involved, comparison operators, and acceptable value ranges. Consider any dependencies or interdependencies between rules and ensure that the rules align with your organization's data governance policies.

Configure Rule Framework: In SAP MDG, the Business Rules Framework Plus (BRF+) provides the platform for defining and implementing business rules. Configure the BRF+ framework according to your organization's requirements. Set up rule sets, rule applications, and conditions within the framework.

Section 5.2: Configuring Validations and Derivations

Validations and derivations are essential components of SAP MDG that help enforce data integrity and automate data population. Let's explore the steps involved in configuring validations and derivations.

Validation Rules: Define validation rules to ensure that master data records adhere to predefined data quality standards. Determine which attributes require validation checks and specify the validation criteria. Configure checks such as mandatory fields, data format validations, or value range validations. Implement validation rules to prevent incorrect or incomplete data entry.

Derivation Rules: Derivation rules automatically populate certain fields based on predefined logic or values from other fields. Determine the fields that need to be derived and establish the rules for their population. Configure the derivation logic, considering any dependencies or data transformations required. Derivations can simplify data entry, reduce manual effort, and ensure consistent data across master data records.

Rule Activation: Once the validations and derivations are defined, activate the rules within SAP MDG. Ensure that the rules are enabled and active in the relevant master data processes. Test the rules thoroughly to verify their correctness and effectiveness.

Section 5.3: Enforcing Data Governance Policies and Standards

SAP MDG enables the enforcement of data governance policies and standards through the implementation of business rules and validations. Here are some key considerations for effectively enforcing data governance:

Rule Execution Sequence: Define the order of rule execution to ensure that business rules and validations are performed in the appropriate sequence. Consider any dependencies or interdependencies between rules and configure the execution sequence accordingly. This ensures that the correct data governance policies are enforced and that data quality is maintained.

Error Handling and Notifications: SAP MDG allows you to configure error handling mechanisms for business rule violations and validation failures. Determine how errors or violations should be handled, such as displaying error messages, blocking data entry, or triggering notifications to data stewards or responsible parties. Implement appropriate error handling and notification mechanisms to ensure timely resolution of issues.

Exception Handling: Define exception handling procedures for scenarios where data does not comply with the predefined rules or standards. Identify the necessary actions to be taken in case of exceptions, such as manual review, data cleansing, or exception approvals. Implement exception handling workflows or processes to address data anomalies effectively.

Data Governance Policies: Document and communicate data governance policies and standards to all relevant stakeholders. Ensure that the implemented business rules and validations align with these policies. Regularly review and update the policies as needed to reflect changes in regulatory requirements or organizational needs.

In Chapter 6, we will explore user interfaces and the data governance framework in SAP MDG. We will discuss the different user interfaces available, customization options, and how to implement the data governance framework. Stay tuned for Chapter 6: User Interfaces and Data Governance Framework.

Chapter 6: User Interfaces and Data Governance Framework

Section 6.1: Exploring the SAP MDG User Interfaces

SAP Master Data Governance (MDG) provides user-friendly interfaces for different user roles involved in master data management. In this chapter, we will explore the various user interfaces available in SAP MDG and their functionalities.

Web-based UI: The web-based user interface in SAP MDG offers a browser-based interface accessible from any device with a web browser. It provides a comprehensive set of features for creating, editing, and reviewing master data records. Users can navigate through different screens, enter data, and perform data validations using the web UI.

Fiori Apps: SAP MDG also offers Fiori apps that provide a simplified and intuitive user experience. These apps are built on the SAP Fiori design principles and can be accessed from desktops, tablets, or mobile devices. Fiori apps offer specific functionalities for tasks such as data creation, approval workflows, or data quality monitoring.

Data Quality Dashboards: SAP MDG provides data quality dashboards to monitor the quality of master data. These dashboards display key data quality metrics, such as completeness, accuracy, or consistency, in a visual format. Users can drill down into specific data sets or records to identify and resolve data quality issues.

Section 6.2: Customizing UIs and Creating Data Quality Dashboards

SAP MDG allows customization of user interfaces to meet specific business requirements and enhance user experience. Let's explore the customization options available for UIs and the creation of data quality dashboards.

UI Configuration: Customize the web-based UI and Fiori apps to align with your organization's branding and usability guidelines. Modify the layout, color schemes, or logos to provide a consistent user experience. Tailor the UI screens to display relevant fields, sections, or tabs based on user roles or business process requirements.

UI Personalization: Enable users to personalize their UI settings by allowing them to rearrange fields, customize views, or save personal preferences. Personalization options enhance user productivity and satisfaction by providing a tailored and efficient working environment.

Data Quality Dashboards: Configure data quality dashboards to visualize key data quality metrics. Define the metrics and thresholds that are important for your organization's data governance goals. Customize the dashboard layout and design to present the metrics in a meaningful and easily understandable format. Implement drill-down capabilities to investigate data quality issues at a granular level.

Section 6.3: Implementing the Data Governance Framework

The data governance framework in SAP MDG provides the structure and processes to enforce data governance policies and standards. Let's explore the key steps involved in implementing the data governance framework.

Data Governance Policies: Review and finalize the data governance policies that align with your organization's objectives and regulatory requirements. Define the rules, guidelines, and standards for data creation, maintenance, and validation. Document these policies and ensure that they are communicated and understood by all relevant stakeholders.

User Roles and Authorizations: Define user roles and authorizations in SAP MDG based on the data governance policies and processes. Assign roles to users based on their responsibilities and access requirements. Implement authorization controls to ensure that users have appropriate access to perform their assigned tasks.

Workflow and Approval Processes: Configure workflow and approval processes in SAP MDG to align with the data governance policies. Define the sequence of approval steps, responsible approvers, and decision points. Configure the workflows to enforce the defined rules and ensure that master data changes undergo the required review and approval.

Data Stewardship: Identify data stewards or data governance teams responsible for overseeing data quality, consistency, and compliance. Define their roles, responsibilities, and tasks within the data governance framework. Establish communication channels and escalation procedures for data stewardship activities.

In Chapter 7, we will explore data quality management in SAP MDG. We will discuss data quality rules, data cleansing, enrichment techniques, and monitoring and reporting on data quality. Stay tuned for Chapter 7: Data Quality Management.

Chapter 7: Data Quality Management

Section 7.1: Introduction to Data Quality Management

Data quality is a critical aspect of effective master data governance. In this chapter, we will explore data quality management in SAP Master Data Governance (MDG) and the processes involved in ensuring high-quality master data.

Importance of Data Quality: Data quality directly impacts the accuracy, reliability, and effectiveness of master data. Poor data quality can lead to incorrect business decisions, operational inefficiencies, and compliance issues. Data quality management in SAP MDG aims to improve data accuracy, completeness, consistency, and timeliness.

Data Quality Metrics: Define key data quality metrics that align with your organization's data governance objectives. Common data quality metrics include completeness, accuracy, consistency, uniqueness, and timeliness. These metrics serve as benchmarks to evaluate the quality of master data.

Section 7.2: Setting Up Data Quality Rules and Checks

Data quality rules and checks form the foundation of data quality management in SAP MDG. Let's explore the steps involved in setting up data quality rules and checks.

Identify Data Quality Rules: Analyze your master data and identify areas where data quality issues are prevalent. Based on these findings, define data quality rules that address these issues. For example, you can define rules to check for missing values, invalid formats, or inconsistent data across attributes.

Configure Data Quality Checks: In SAP MDG, set up data quality checks to enforce the defined rules. Determine the attributes and conditions on which the checks will be performed. Configure checks such as mandatory fields, data format validations, value range validations, or referential integrity checks.

Error Handling: Specify the actions to be taken when data quality checks fail. Define error handling procedures, such as displaying error messages, blocking data entry, or triggering notifications to data stewards. Implement appropriate error handling mechanisms to ensure timely resolution of data quality issues.

Section 7.3: Data Cleansing and Enrichment Techniques

Data cleansing and enrichment are essential processes to improve the quality of master data. Let's explore the techniques involved in data cleansing and enrichment in SAP MDG.

Data Cleansing: SAP MDG provides data cleansing functionality to rectify data quality issues. Identify common data quality problems such as duplicate records, inconsistent formats, or incomplete values. Utilize data cleansing techniques such as standardization, deduplication, and data enrichment to resolve these issues.

Data Enrichment: Enhance master data by enriching it with additional information. SAP MDG allows integration with external data sources or third-party providers to retrieve additional data. This can include address validation, geocoding, or enrichment with industry-specific data. Implement data enrichment strategies to improve the completeness and accuracy of master data.

Section 7.4: Monitoring and Reporting on Data Quality

Monitoring and reporting are crucial for assessing the effectiveness of data quality management efforts. Let's explore the processes involved in monitoring and reporting on data quality in SAP MDG.

Data Quality Monitoring: Utilize the data quality monitoring features in SAP MDG to track the quality of master data over time. Monitor the defined data quality metrics and identify trends or patterns. Regularly assess data quality to proactively identify and resolve data quality issues.

Data Quality Reporting: SAP MDG offers reporting capabilities to generate data quality reports and metrics. Define the key performance indicators (KPIs) that reflect your data quality objectives. Generate reports to visualize data quality metrics and trends. Analyze the reports to identify areas for improvement and track the effectiveness of data quality management initiatives.

In Chapter 8, we will explore integration and extensibility in SAP MDG. We will discuss how to integrate SAP MDG with other systems, extend its functionality, and enhance user interfaces. Stay tuned for Chapter 8: Integration and Extensibility.

Chapter 8: Integration and Extensibility

Section 8.1: Integration with Other Systems

SAP Master Data Governance (MDG) can be integrated with various systems to ensure data consistency and synchronization across the enterprise landscape. In this chapter, we will explore the integration capabilities of SAP MDG and the processes involved.

Identify Integration Requirements: Determine the systems that need to be integrated with SAP MDG. These can include other SAP systems, such as SAP ERP or SAP CRM, as well as non-SAP systems. Identify the master data objects and processes that require integration to maintain data consistency.

Integration Technologies: SAP MDG supports various integration technologies, such as BAPIs (Business Application Programming Interfaces), IDocs (Intermediate Documents), and web services. Select the appropriate integration technology based on your system landscape and integration requirements.

Data Replication: Configure data replication settings to synchronize master data between SAP MDG and the integrated systems. Define the frequency and direction of data replication. Specify the mapping and transformation rules to ensure the data is correctly transferred and mapped to the target system.

Integration Testing: Conduct thorough integration testing to ensure that the data replication and synchronization processes function as intended. Validate the data flow and consistency between SAP MDG and the integrated systems. Address any issues or discrepancies identified during testing.

Section 8.2: Extending SAP MDG Functionality

SAP MDG provides extensibility options to enhance its functionality and meet specific business requirements. Let's explore the processes involved in extending SAP MDG.

Identify Extension Requirements: Identify the areas where you require additional functionality or customizations in SAP MDG. Determine the specific business requirements that necessitate extension.

Custom Fields and UI Enhancements: SAP MDG allows the addition of custom fields to capture additional data not available in the standard data model. Identify the fields required for your business processes and add them as extension fields. Customize the user interfaces to include these custom fields and provide an enhanced user experience.

Custom Business Rules: Implement custom business rules and validations to enforce specific data governance policies or additional checks. Define the conditions, actions, and evaluation logic for the custom rules. Configure the rule framework in SAP MDG to include these custom rules.

Enhancements through ABAP Development: SAP MDG allows for ABAP (Advanced Business Application Programming) development to implement complex customizations and extensions. Leverage ABAP programming to enhance the functionality of SAP MDG, integrate with external systems, or implement specific business processes.

Section 8.3: Enhancing User Interfaces

SAP MDG offers customization options to enhance the user interfaces and improve user experience. Let's explore the processes involved in enhancing the user interfaces.

UI Customization: Customize the web-based UI and Fiori apps to align with your organization's branding and user preferences. Modify the layout, color schemes, or logos to provide a consistent user experience. Tailor the UI screens to display relevant fields, sections, or tabs based on user roles or business process requirements.

Fiori App Extensions: SAP MDG provides extensibility options for Fiori apps. Leverage these extensions to add additional functionalities, screens, or actions to the Fiori apps. Enhance the user interfaces by incorporating custom logic, workflows, or data validations.

User Experience Design: Consider user experience design principles when customizing the user interfaces. Aim for simplicity, clarity, and intuitiveness in the UI layouts and interactions. Conduct user testing and gather feedback to iteratively improve the user experience.

In Chapter 9, we will explore master data consolidation and harmonization in SAP MDG. We will discuss the processes involved in identifying duplicates, resolving conflicts, and establishing a single version of truth for master data. Stay tuned for Chapter 9: Master Data Consolidation and Harmonization.

Chapter 9: Master Data Consolidation and Harmonization

Section 9.1: Importance of Master Data Consolidation and Harmonization

Master data consolidation and harmonization are crucial processes in SAP Master Data Governance (MDG) that aim to establish a single, consistent, and reliable version of master data across the enterprise. In this chapter, we will explore the importance of master data consolidation and harmonization and the benefits they bring to organizations.

Data Consistency: Master data consolidation ensures that there is a consistent representation of master data across different systems and applications. It eliminates duplicate or conflicting data entries, reducing data discrepancies and improving data quality.

Single Version of Truth: Consolidating master data helps organizations establish a single version of truth for their data. By eliminating duplicates and resolving conflicts, organizations can rely on accurate and consistent master data for their decision-making processes.

Enhanced Efficiency: Consolidated master data reduces the complexity and redundancy of data management processes. It streamlines data entry, maintenance, and reporting activities, leading to improved operational efficiency and productivity.

Improved Analytics and Reporting: Consolidated and harmonized master data provides a solid foundation for accurate analytics and reporting. It enables organizations to generate reliable insights, perform meaningful data analysis, and make informed business decisions based on accurate and consistent data.

Section 9.2: Identifying Duplicate Master Data Records

Identifying duplicate master data records is a critical step in the master data consolidation process. Let's explore the techniques and processes involved in identifying duplicates.

Data Profiling: Conduct data profiling activities to gain an understanding of the quality and structure of your master data. Analyze data patterns, variations, and inconsistencies to identify potential duplicate records.

Data Matching: Utilize data matching techniques to compare master data records and identify potential duplicates. Consider various matching algorithms, such as exact match, fuzzy match, or phonetic match, depending on the data attributes and quality requirements.

Duplicate Detection Rules: Define duplicate detection rules in SAP MDG based on the matching criteria and business requirements. Configure the rules to identify potential duplicates based on selected attributes and comparison logic.

Duplicate Detection Process: Execute the duplicate detection process in SAP MDG to identify potential duplicates within the master data. Review the identified duplicates and validate their accuracy before proceeding to the next steps.

Section 9.3: Resolving Duplicate and Conflicting Data

Once duplicate master data records are identified, the next step is to resolve them and establish a single version of truth. Let's explore the techniques and processes involved in resolving duplicates and conflicting data.

Data Comparison: Compare the duplicate records to identify the conflicting data elements. Evaluate the differences and determine the most accurate and reliable data values.

Survivorship Rules: Define survivorship rules to determine which data values should be selected as the "survivor" or preferred values. Consider factors such as data quality, data source reliability, or business rules to establish the survivorship criteria.

Merge and Consolidate: Merge the duplicate records, taking into account the survivorship rules. Update the duplicate records with the preferred data values and consolidate them into a single, accurate master data record.

Data Validation: Perform data validation checks on the merged and consolidated master data records to ensure data quality and integrity. Verify that the resolved data aligns with the defined business rules and validation criteria.

Section 9.4: Establishing Data Governance for Master Data

Establishing effective data governance is essential for maintaining the integrity and consistency of master data. Let's explore the key steps involved in establishing data governance for master data consolidation and harmonization.

Data Governance Framework: Define a comprehensive data governance framework that outlines the policies, roles, responsibilities, and processes for master data management. Ensure that the framework addresses data consolidation and harmonization requirements.

Data Stewardship: Assign data stewards or data governance teams responsible for overseeing master data consolidation and harmonization activities. Define their roles, responsibilities, and tasks within the data governance framework. Establish communication channels and escalation procedures for data stewardship.

Data Governance Policies: Document and communicate data governance policies and standards related to master data consolidation and harmonization. Ensure that the policies are aligned with industry best practices and regulatory requirements.

Data Governance Processes: Implement data governance processes for master data consolidation and harmonization. Define the workflows, approval mechanisms, and escalation procedures required to ensure the accuracy and reliability of master data.

In Chapter 10, we will explore data migration strategies in SAP MDG. We will discuss the processes involved in migrating master data from legacy systems to SAP MDG and ensuring data integrity and consistency. Stay tuned for Chapter 10: Data Migration Strategies.

Chapter 10: Data Migration Strategies

Section 10.1: Introduction to Data Migration in SAP MDG

Data migration is a crucial step when implementing SAP Master Data Governance (MDG) as it involves transferring master data from legacy systems to SAP MDG. In this chapter, we will explore the strategies and processes involved in data migration to ensure data integrity and consistency.

Importance of Data Migration: Data migration is essential to ensure a smooth transition from legacy systems to SAP MDG. It involves transferring master data accurately and efficiently while maintaining data quality and consistency.

Data Migration Challenges: Data migration can pose several challenges, including data mapping, data cleansing, data transformation, and ensuring data quality. Planning and implementing an effective data migration strategy are key to overcoming these challenges.

Section 10.2: Data Migration Planning

Effective planning is critical for a successful data migration process. Let's explore the key steps involved in data migration planning.

Define Migration Scope: Determine the scope of the data migration by identifying the master data objects and attributes that need to be migrated to SAP MDG. Consider the data volume, complexity, and dependencies among different master data entities.

Data Mapping: Perform data mapping to identify the mapping between the legacy system's data structure and the target SAP MDG data model. Determine the mapping rules, field transformations, and data conversion requirements. Develop a comprehensive data mapping document as a reference during the migration process.

Data Cleansing and Transformation: Assess the quality of legacy data and define data cleansing and transformation rules. Identify and rectify any data quality issues, such as duplicates, incomplete or inconsistent data, or invalid formats. Transform the data to meet the requirements of the SAP MDG data model.

Data Extraction and Preparation: Extract the data from the legacy systems using suitable extraction methods, such as data export or database queries. Cleanse and transform the extracted data according to the defined rules and requirements. Prepare the data for loading into SAP MDG.

Section 10.3: Data Migration Execution

Once the planning phase is complete, it's time to execute the data migration process. Let's explore the key steps involved in executing data migration in SAP MDG.

Data Load: Load the cleansed and transformed data into SAP MDG. Utilize the appropriate data loading mechanisms provided by SAP MDG, such as direct table insert, BAPIs, or IDocs. Ensure that the data is loaded accurately and matches the defined data mapping and transformation rules.

Data Validation: Perform data validation checks after the data load to ensure the accuracy and integrity of the migrated data. Verify that the migrated data aligns with the defined data quality rules and validation criteria. Address any data quality issues identified during the validation process.

Data Reconciliation: Reconcile the migrated data in SAP MDG with the source data in the legacy systems. Conduct thorough checks to ensure that the migrated data accurately represents the original data. Resolve any discrepancies or data mismatches identified during the reconciliation process.

Post-Migration Activities: After the data migration, perform post-migration activities such as data verification, user acceptance testing, and data consistency checks. Ensure that the migrated data is functioning as expected and is consistent with the business requirements.

Section 10.4: Data Migration Best Practices

Adhering to best practices can help ensure a successful data migration process. Let's explore some best practices to consider during data migration in SAP MDG.

Data Quality Assessment: Conduct a thorough assessment of the quality of legacy data before the migration process. Identify data quality issues, such as duplicates, inconsistencies, or incomplete data. Address these issues through data cleansing and transformation activities.

Data Migration Testing: Perform comprehensive testing of the data migration process to validate its accuracy and completeness. Develop test scenarios, data sets, and scripts to simulate different migration scenarios. Execute end-to-end tests and address any issues identified during the testing phase.

Data Governance Alignment: Ensure that the migrated data aligns with the established data governance policies and standards. Validate that the data meets the defined data quality rules, business rules, and validation criteria.

Data Migration Documentation: Document the data migration processes, including the migration strategy, data mapping, transformation rules, and validation procedures. This documentation serves as a reference for future data migration activities and provides a record of the migration process.

In Chapter 11, we will explore data maintenance and ongoing data governance in SAP MDG. We will discuss the processes involved in data maintenance, data quality monitoring, and data governance activities to ensure the ongoing integrity and consistency of master data. Stay tuned for Chapter 11: Data Maintenance and Ongoing Data Governance.

Chapter 11: Data Maintenance and Ongoing Data Governance

Section 11.1: Introduction to Data Maintenance in SAP MDG

Data maintenance is a crucial aspect of SAP Master Data Governance (MDG) that ensures the ongoing integrity and consistency of master data. In this chapter, we will explore the processes involved in data maintenance and ongoing data governance in SAP MDG.

Importance of Data Maintenance: Data maintenance involves the regular updates, corrections, and monitoring of master data to ensure its accuracy, completeness, and consistency. It is essential to keep master data up to date and aligned with the evolving business requirements and data governance policies.

Data Governance Continuum: Data maintenance is an integral part of the broader data governance continuum. It involves activities such as data quality monitoring, data enrichment, data validation, and data lifecycle management to ensure ongoing data integrity and compliance.

Section 11.2: Data Maintenance Processes

Let's explore the key processes involved in data maintenance in SAP MDG.

Data Entry and Modification: Users can create new master data records or modify existing records through the user interfaces provided by SAP MDG. They can enter data, update attributes, and maintain the relevant information required for each master data object.

Approval Workflows: Data maintenance processes often involve approval workflows to ensure proper authorization and control over master data changes. Configure workflows in SAP MDG to enforce approval steps, decision points, and notifications for data modifications.

Data Validation: Perform data validation checks during data maintenance to ensure the accuracy and consistency of master data. Configure validation rules in SAP MDG to enforce data quality standards, such as mandatory fields, value checks, or data format validations.

Data Enrichment: Data maintenance also includes data enrichment activities to enhance master data with additional information. Users can leverage data enrichment functionality in SAP MDG to retrieve data from external sources, integrate with third-party providers, or incorporate industry-specific data.

Section 11.3: Data Quality Monitoring and Reporting

Data quality monitoring and reporting are vital for ensuring ongoing data integrity and compliance. Let's explore the processes involved in data quality monitoring and reporting in SAP MDG.

Data Quality Metrics: Define key data quality metrics and indicators that reflect your organization's data governance objectives. Examples include completeness, accuracy, consistency, uniqueness, and timeliness. These metrics serve as benchmarks to assess the quality of master data.

Data Quality Monitoring: Utilize the data quality monitoring features in SAP MDG to track and monitor the defined data quality metrics. Generate reports and dashboards to visualize data quality trends, anomalies, and exceptions. Regularly assess data quality to identify areas for improvement and address any data quality issues.

Data Quality Reporting: SAP MDG provides reporting capabilities to generate data quality reports and metrics. Customize reports to display the relevant data quality metrics and trends. Analyze the reports to identify patterns, root causes of data quality issues, and areas requiring data governance interventions.

Section 11.4: Data Lifecycle Management

Data lifecycle management involves managing the different stages of master data from creation to retirement. Let's explore the processes involved in data lifecycle management in SAP MDG.

Data Creation: Configure data creation processes in SAP MDG to ensure that new master data records are created following defined business rules and data governance policies. Define default values, data entry templates, and validation rules to enforce data quality and consistency during data creation.

Data Modification: Data modification processes enable users to update existing master data records. Implement controls and workflows to govern data modifications, ensuring proper authorization and adherence to data governance policies.

Data Archiving and Retention: Define data archiving and retention policies to manage the lifecycle of master data. Implement archiving processes to remove inactive or obsolete data from the active system. Define retention periods for different master data objects based on regulatory requirements and business needs.

Data Purging: Implement data purging processes to permanently remove master data records that have exceeded their retention period or are no longer required. Ensure that data purging activities comply with legal and regulatory obligations.

In Chapter 12, we will explore data migration strategies in SAP MDG. We will discuss the processes involved in migrating master data from legacy systems to SAP MDG and ensuring data integrity and consistency. Stay tuned for Chapter 12: Data Migration Strategies.

Chapter 12: Data Migration Strategies

Section 12.1: Introduction to Data Migration in SAP MDG

Data migration is a critical process when implementing SAP Master Data Governance (MDG) as it involves transferring master data from legacy systems to SAP MDG. In this chapter, we will explore the strategies and best practices involved in data migration to ensure data integrity and consistency.

Importance of Data Migration: Data migration is essential to ensure a smooth transition from legacy systems to SAP MDG. It involves transferring master data accurately and efficiently while maintaining data quality and consistency.

Data Migration Challenges: Data migration can pose several challenges, including data mapping, data cleansing, data transformation, and ensuring data quality. Planning and implementing an effective data migration strategy are key to overcoming these challenges.

Section 12.2: Data Migration Planning

Effective planning is crucial for a successful data migration process. Let's explore the key steps involved in data migration planning.

Define Migration Scope: Determine the scope of the data migration by identifying the master data objects and attributes that need to be migrated to SAP MDG. Consider the data volume, complexity, and dependencies among different master data entities.

Data Mapping: Perform data mapping to identify the mapping between the legacy system's data structure and the target SAP MDG data model. Determine the mapping rules, field transformations, and data conversion requirements. Develop a comprehensive data mapping document as a reference during the migration process.

Data Cleansing and Transformation: Assess the quality of legacy data and define data cleansing and transformation rules. Identify and rectify any data quality issues, such as duplicates, incomplete or inconsistent data, or invalid formats. Transform the data to meet the requirements of the SAP MDG data model.

Data Extraction and Preparation: Extract the data from the legacy systems using suitable extraction methods, such as data export or database queries. Cleanse and transform the extracted data according to the defined rules and requirements. Prepare the data for loading into SAP MDG.

Section 12.3: Data Migration Execution

Once the planning phase is complete, it's time to execute the data migration process. Let's explore the key steps involved in executing data migration in SAP MDG.

Data Load: Load the cleansed and transformed data into SAP MDG. Utilize the appropriate data loading mechanisms provided by SAP MDG, such as direct table insert, BAPIs, or IDocs. Ensure that the data is loaded accurately and matches the defined data mapping and transformation rules.

Data Validation: Perform data validation checks after the data load to ensure the accuracy and integrity of the migrated data. Verify that the migrated data aligns with the defined data quality rules and validation criteria. Address any data quality issues identified during the validation process.

Data Reconciliation: Reconcile the migrated data in SAP MDG with the source data in the legacy systems. Conduct thorough checks to ensure that the migrated data accurately represents the original data. Resolve any discrepancies or data mismatches identified during the reconciliation process.

Post-Migration Activities: After the data migration, perform post-migration activities such as data verification, user acceptance testing, and data consistency checks. Ensure that the migrated data is functioning as expected and is consistent with the business requirements.

Section 12.4: Data Migration Best Practices

Adhering to best practices can help ensure a successful data migration process. Let's explore some best practices to consider during data migration in SAP MDG.

Data Quality Assessment: Conduct a thorough assessment of the quality of legacy data before the migration process. Identify data quality issues, such as duplicates, inconsistencies, or incomplete data. Address these issues through data cleansing and transformation activities.

Data Migration Testing: Perform comprehensive testing of the data migration process to validate its accuracy and completeness. Develop test scenarios, data sets, and scripts to simulate different migration scenarios. Execute end-to-end tests and address any issues identified during the testing phase.

Data Governance Alignment: Ensure that the migrated data aligns with the established data governance policies and standards. Validate that the data meets the defined data quality rules, business rules, and validation criteria.

Data Migration Documentation: Document the data migration processes, including the migration strategy, data mapping, transformation rules, and validation procedures. This documentation serves as a reference for future data migration activities and provides a record of the migration process.

In Chapter 13, we will explore reporting and analytics in SAP MDG. We will discuss the reporting capabilities, analytics features, and data visualization options available to gain insights from master data in SAP MDG. Stay tuned for Chapter 13: Reporting and Analytics.

Chapter 13: Reporting and Analytics

Section 13.1: Introduction to Reporting and Analytics in SAP MDG

Reporting and analytics are essential components of SAP Master Data Governance (MDG) that provide insights into master data and support data-driven decision-making. In this chapter, we will explore the reporting capabilities, analytics features, and data visualization options available in SAP MDG.

Importance of Reporting and Analytics: Reporting and analytics enable organizations to gain valuable insights from master data. They help identify trends, patterns, and anomalies, and provide data-driven intelligence for strategic decision-making, performance monitoring, and continuous improvement.

Data Visualization: Data visualization is a key aspect of reporting and analytics in SAP MDG. It involves presenting data in graphical or visual formats, such as charts, graphs, and dashboards, to enhance understanding and facilitate data exploration.

Section 13.2: Reporting in SAP MDG

Let's explore the reporting capabilities available in SAP MDG.

Standard Reports: SAP MDG provides a range of standard reports that offer pre-defined views and insights into master data. These reports cover various aspects of master data, such as data completeness, data quality metrics, or data change history. Users can access these reports to gain valuable insights into their master data.

Ad-Hoc Reporting: SAP MDG allows users to create ad-hoc reports to meet specific reporting requirements. Users can define their own report layouts, data selection criteria, and output formats. Ad-hoc reporting empowers users to extract and analyze master data based on their unique needs.

Data Extraction and Export: SAP MDG provides data extraction and export functionalities that enable users to extract master data and export it to other tools or systems for further analysis. Users can export data in various formats, such as Excel, CSV, or PDF, to perform in-depth analysis using external reporting tools.

Section 13.3: Analytics and Data Visualization

Let's explore the analytics features and data visualization options available in SAP MDG.

SAP Analytics Cloud Integration: SAP MDG integrates with SAP Analytics Cloud, a powerful analytics platform that enables advanced data visualization, predictive analytics, and machine learning capabilities. Users can leverage SAP Analytics Cloud to create interactive dashboards, perform advanced analytics, and gain deeper insights from master data.

Data Visualization Tools: SAP MDG supports data visualization tools such as SAP Lumira and SAP BusinessObjects Web Intelligence, which allow users to create visually appealing and interactive reports and dashboards. These tools provide rich visualization options, including charts, graphs, heat maps, and geo-mapping, to facilitate data exploration and analysis.

Key Performance Indicators (KPIs): SAP MDG allows users to define and track key performance indicators (KPIs) to monitor data quality, compliance, and process efficiency. KPIs provide a quick snapshot of the health and performance of master data and support data-driven decision-making.

Section 13.4: Advanced Analytics and Predictive Insights

Let's explore the advanced analytics and predictive insights capabilities available in SAP MDG.

Predictive Data Quality: SAP MDG offers predictive data quality capabilities that help identify potential data quality issues before they occur. Predictive analytics techniques, such as machine learning algorithms, can analyze historical data patterns and predict data quality anomalies or errors.

Data Profiling and Segmentation: SAP MDG supports data profiling and segmentation techniques that enable users to analyze master data based on specific criteria or attributes. These techniques help identify data patterns, segment data subsets, and uncover hidden insights within the master data.

Predictive Maintenance: SAP MDG can be integrated with other SAP solutions, such as SAP Predictive Maintenance and Service (PdMS), to enable predictive maintenance capabilities. By leveraging machine learning and predictive analytics, organizations can proactively identify maintenance needs, optimize asset performance, and reduce downtime.

In Chapter 14, we will explore the integration of SAP MDG with other SAP solutions and systems. We will discuss the integration possibilities, benefits, and best practices for integrating SAP MDG with other SAP modules and external systems. Stay tuned for Chapter 14: Integration with Other Systems.

Chapter 14: Integration with Other Systems

Section 14.1: Introduction to Integration with Other Systems

Integration is a critical aspect of SAP Master Data Governance (MDG) that ensures data consistency and synchronization across various systems. In this chapter, we will explore the integration possibilities, benefits, and best practices for integrating SAP MDG with other SAP modules and external systems.

Importance of Integration: Integrating SAP MDG with other systems allows for seamless data exchange, eliminates data silos, and ensures consistent master data across the enterprise. Integration enhances operational efficiency, data accuracy, and business process alignment.

Integration Scenarios: SAP MDG can be integrated with various SAP modules, such as SAP ERP, SAP CRM, or SAP S/4HANA, to streamline master data management processes. Additionally, it can be integrated with external systems, such as third-party applications or data providers, to enrich master data or synchronize data with external sources.

Section 14.2: Integration with SAP Modules

Let's explore the integration possibilities and best practices for integrating SAP MDG with other SAP modules.

Integration with SAP ERP: Integration with SAP ERP ensures the synchronization of master data between SAP MDG and SAP ERP, enabling consistent data across both systems. Best practices include defining mapping rules, establishing data replication processes, and implementing change management strategies.

Integration with SAP CRM: Integrating SAP MDG with SAP CRM allows for unified customer master data management. It enables the synchronization of customer data between the two systems, ensuring a single view of customers across the organization. Best practices include mapping customer data fields, establishing data replication processes, and implementing data consistency checks.

Integration with SAP S/4HANA: Integration with SAP S/4HANA enables unified master data management across the enterprise. It ensures consistent and synchronized data between SAP MDG and SAP S/4HANA, supporting streamlined business processes. Best practices include leveraging integration technologies such as IDocs or APIs, mapping data structures, and establishing data replication mechanisms.

Section 14.3: Integration with External Systems

Let's explore the integration possibilities and best practices for integrating SAP MDG with external systems.

Data Enrichment: Integrate SAP MDG with external data providers or third-party applications to enrich master data with additional information. This can include address validation, geocoding, industry-specific data, or compliance data. Best practices include establishing data mapping rules, configuring integration interfaces, and ensuring data consistency during the integration process.

Data Synchronization: Integrate SAP MDG with external systems to synchronize master data with external sources. This can involve bidirectional data exchange, ensuring that changes made in SAP MDG are reflected in the external systems and vice versa. Best practices include defining data mapping rules, implementing data replication processes, and performing data consistency checks.

API Integration: Leverage APIs (Application Programming Interfaces) to integrate SAP MDG with external systems. APIs provide a standardized and secure way to exchange data between systems. Best practices include designing robust API interfaces, implementing authentication and authorization mechanisms, and establishing error handling and data validation processes.

Section 14.4: Best Practices for Integration

Let's explore some best practices for successful integration with SAP MDG.

Data Mapping and Transformation: Define clear data mapping rules and transformation logic to ensure seamless data exchange between systems. Validate data mapping rules to ensure accurate and consistent data integration.

Data Replication Processes: Establish reliable and efficient data replication processes to synchronize master data between systems. Define the frequency, direction, and scope of data replication. Implement data validation and reconciliation mechanisms to maintain data integrity.

Change Management: Implement change management practices to handle data changes and updates in a controlled manner. Establish governance processes, such as change control boards and approval workflows, to ensure proper authorization and documentation of data changes.

Data Consistency Checks: Implement data consistency checks during the integration process to identify and resolve any data discrepancies or conflicts. Perform regular data validation and reconciliation to ensure the consistency and accuracy of master data across integrated systems.

In Chapter 15, we will discuss best practices for SAP MDG implementation and deployment. We will explore key considerations, project planning, and strategies to ensure a successful implementation of SAP MDG within an organization. Stay tuned for Chapter 15: Implementation and Deployment Best Practices.

Chapter 15: Implementation and Deployment Best Practices

Section 15.1: Introduction to SAP MDG Implementation and Deployment

Implementing and deploying SAP Master Data Governance (MDG) requires careful planning and execution to ensure a successful implementation. In this chapter, we will explore the best practices, key considerations, and strategies for implementing and deploying SAP MDG within an organization.

Importance of Implementation and Deployment: Effective implementation and deployment of SAP MDG is crucial to realize the full potential of the solution. It ensures smooth adoption, aligns with business requirements, and maximizes the benefits of centralized master data management.

Project Planning and Management: Thorough project planning is essential for a successful SAP MDG implementation. It involves defining project objectives, timelines, resource allocation, and risk management strategies. Establishing a dedicated project team and adopting proven project management methodologies will contribute to a successful implementation.

Section 15.2: Key Considerations for SAP MDG Implementation

Let's explore the key considerations to keep in mind during SAP MDG implementation.

Business Process Analysis: Conduct a comprehensive analysis of existing business processes related to master data management. Identify pain points, inefficiencies, and areas for improvement. Use this analysis to define the future state processes that align with the capabilities of SAP MDG.

Data Governance Framework: Establish a robust data governance framework that aligns with the organization's data management strategy and business goals. Define data governance policies, roles, responsibilities, and processes. Ensure that the data governance framework supports the objectives of SAP MDG implementation.

Data Quality Assessment: Perform a thorough assessment of the quality of existing master data. Identify data quality issues, such as duplicates, inconsistencies, or incomplete data. Develop a data cleansing and data enrichment strategy to address these issues during the implementation process.

Change Management and User Adoption: Plan for change management activities to facilitate user adoption and ensure smooth transition to SAP MDG. Involve key stakeholders and end-users throughout the implementation process. Provide training, documentation, and support to help users understand the benefits and effectively use SAP MDG.

Section 15.3: Implementation Strategies and Best Practices

Let's explore some implementation strategies and best practices for SAP MDG.

Phased Approach: Consider adopting a phased approach for the implementation, focusing on specific master data objects, business units, or processes. This approach allows for incremental adoption and reduces the complexity of the implementation.

Data Migration Strategy: Develop a comprehensive data migration strategy to ensure the accurate and efficient transfer of master data from legacy systems to SAP MDG. Consider data mapping, data cleansing, and data validation techniques to ensure data integrity during the migration process.

Customization and Configuration: Strike a balance between customization and configuration. Leverage the standard functionalities of SAP MDG as much as possible to minimize complexity and simplify future upgrades. Customize only when necessary to meet specific business requirements.

Testing and Quality Assurance: Implement a robust testing and quality assurance process to validate the functionality, data accuracy, and system performance of SAP MDG. Perform comprehensive testing, including unit testing, integration testing, and user acceptance testing, to ensure the system meets business requirements.

Section 15.4: Continuous Improvement and Optimization

Once SAP MDG is deployed, continuous improvement and optimization are crucial for maximizing its benefits. Let's explore some best practices for continuous improvement.

Performance Monitoring: Establish key performance indicators (KPIs) to monitor the performance of SAP MDG. Regularly analyze the KPIs to identify areas for improvement and take proactive measures to optimize system performance.

User Feedback and Engagement: Encourage user feedback and engagement to gather insights and suggestions for system enhancements. Conduct periodic surveys, feedback sessions, and user forums to understand user needs and expectations. Incorporate user feedback into future system enhancements.

Ongoing Data Governance: Maintain a strong data governance program even after the SAP MDG implementation. Regularly review and update data governance policies, processes, and standards. Continuously monitor data quality, address data issues, and enforce data governance practices.

System Upgrades and Innovations: Stay up to date with SAP MDG upgrades and new features. Evaluate the new functionalities and innovations introduced by SAP and assess their relevance to your organization. Plan and execute system upgrades to leverage the latest capabilities and enhancements.

By following these best practices and strategies, organizations can successfully implement and deploy SAP MDG, ensuring a streamlined master data management process and realizing the full benefits of centralized data governance.

This concludes our tutorial book on Learn SAP Master Data Governance (MDG). We hope this comprehensive guide has provided you with valuable insights and knowledge to effectively utilize SAP MDG in your organization.